# Sous Vide Cookbook : The Only Sous Vide Recipes Book You Need To Master Sous Vide Cooking.

Amanda Clark.

ISBN: 1547046899
ISBN-13: 9781547046898

# DEDICATION

This humble work wouldn't be alive without my grandma's support, advice and teachings. Grandma, this is for you. I truly appreciate you being part of my life.

# ACKNOWLEDGMENTS

A big thank you to all those who had a hand in the making of this work. Thank you all. You know who you are!

# Introduction:

Cooking can be enjoyable, boring, hard or easy depending on who you are talking to. It is all a matter of opinion. However, there are a number of techniques that can make life easier in the kitchen for all of us, regardless of our beliefs. One such technique is SOUS VIDE COOKING.

## What Is Sous Vide Cooking To Begin With?

The word "sous" is French for "under" and "vide" is French for vacuum, therefore sous vide cooking literally translates to under vacuum cooking. In the traditional method of this type of cooking, food is placed in vacuum sealed pouches (hence the name). In modern times, the vacuum sealed pouches are not necessarily present. Sous vide cooking in the modern context refers to cooking which takes place in a water bath where temperature is controlled extremely precisely and accurately. It is not really a novel concept and has been studied since the early 1900s by food scientists.

## How Is It Different From Traditional Cooking?

Sous vide differs from traditional cooking in two major ways. Firstly, in sharp contrast to traditional cooking, food is sealed in vacuum sealed food grade plastic pouches in sous vide cooking. Secondly, sous vide constitutes extremely precise controlled heating. This is not possible in traditional cooking.

## The Benefits Of Sous Vide Cooking May Be Listed As Follows:

**1) The Food is evenly cooked** : for instance, in a frying pan while cooking fish, the corners are better cooked than the center of the fish. In sous vide this problem does not arise.

**2) The Food is more tender** : sous vide cooking produces food that is more tender.

**3) The Food is more juicy** : this is particularly true for food like chicken. Sous vide extracts juices from them in a way traditional cooking just cannot.

**4) Consistent Results** – the steak will emerge juicy and tender from the vacuum sealed bag every single time.

**5) No need to time** – traditional cooking can offer be cumbersome in that you must time the food to get the best results. In sous vide cooking, this is no longer the case.

Now,

Enough talking about sous vide cooking technique and its benefits. It is time to take the plunge and test the waters yourself. In the pages to come, I listed some of the best sous vide recipes. These are simple, easy and require very little to no time.

With all the love of the world, I wish you an amazing experience with your sous vide recipes.

Amanda

# Chapter 1: Breakfast Recipes

## Eggs With Leek And Salmon

**Servings .4**

**Prep time. 1 minute.**

**cooking time. 75 minutes.**

**Ingredients.**

- 200g cooked salmon.
- 2 medium leeks.
- 4 eggs.
- Unsweetened almond milk.
- Pinch of salt.
- Olive oil.

**Directions.**

- Preheat the cooker to 76 degrees as you blend the eggs and almond milk to mix then keep aside.
- Sauté the leeks in the pan with olive oil for 8 minutes. Transfer and mix with salmons until they're homogeneous. Top with the egg mixture and put in jars then place in a bath to cook for one hour.
- Transfer and serve.

**Nutritional value.**

**Calories 149**

**Protein 12.89g**

**Carbs. 0.77g**

**Fat 9.99g**

# Asparagus And Scrambled Egg

**Servings.4**

**Prep time 5 minutes.**

**Cooking time. 70 minutes.**

**Ingredients.**

- 4 eggs.
- 100g cooked salmon.
- ½ cup cream cheese.
- 4 spears asparagus.
- Olive oil.
- 1tbsp salt.
- ½ cup Crème Fraiche.
- 15g minced shallot.

**Directions.**

- Preheat the cooker to 76.7c.
- Blend together eggs,cheese , salt and cream and set aside. Mix salmon and shallot together in another bowl.
- In 4 jars, pour the egg mixture followed by asparagus and salmon mixture into each. Close the jars and set to cook in the bath for 60 minutes.
- Once ready, reheat and serve.

**Nutritional value.**

**Calories. 189**

**Protein 17.64g**

**Fat 10.1g**

**Carbs 1.43g**

# Sweet Pea Eggs.

**Servings 3**

**Prep time 3 minutes.**

**Cooking time. 65 minutes.**

**Ingredients.**

- 1 cup peas.
- Olive oil
- Salt and pepper.
- 3 eggs.
- 15g shallot.
- ¼ cup creme fraiche.
- ½ cup feta.
- 1tbsp mint.

**Directions.**

- Preheat the cooker to 76C
- Blend eggs with creme,salt,cheese,and eggs.
- Mix the mint, feta, shallot and peas.
- Put the egg mixture into 3 jars and top with the pea mixture. Cover tightly and set to cook in the bath for 1 hour. Transfer and serve.

**Nutritional value.**

**Calories.213**

**Proteins 19g**

**Carbs 6g**

**Fat 11g**

# Cornbread

**Servings 4**

**Prep time 30 minutes.**

**Cooking time 3 hours.**

**Ingredients.**

- 200g cornmeal.
- 100g ready bread dough.
- 4 corn kernels.
- Butter.

**Directions.**

- Preheat the oven to 96 degrees Celsius then grease the canning jars with butter.
- Mix the dough and cornmeal till you get a desired consistency.
- Pour the mixture in 4 canning jars and set to bake for 3 hours.
- Once ready, sit to cool and serve.

**Nutritional value.**

**Calories 145**

**Fat 6g**

**Carbs 19g**

**Protein 4g.**

# Cheese Egg Bites.

**Servings 4.**

**Prep time. 3 minutes**

**Cooking time 1 hour.**

**Ingredients.**

- 4 eggs.
- ½ cup cream cheese.
- Salt.
- ½ cup grated cheese.

**Directions.**

- Preheat the oven to 76C
- Whisk together all ingredients and pour into four jars. Cover appropriately and set for 1 hour.
- Transfer and serve.

**Nutritional value.**

**Calories 134**

**Proteins 12g**

**Fat 9.8g**

**Carbs 1.2g**

# Pumpkin Flans.

**Servings 2**

**Prep time. 30 minutes.**

**Cooking time. 3 hours.**

**Ingredients.**

- 250g pumpkin puree.
- 1 whole egg
- 200ml milk.
- ½ cup pumpkin seeds.
- 4 egg yolks.
- 200mls half and half.
- 1tbsp ginger
- 1tbsp salt.
- 1tbsp rosemary.
- 90g blue cheese.

**Directions.**

- Heat water in the cooker up to 80 degrees. mix all ingredients by whisking them till smooth.
- Pour the mixture into jars and seal them well. Put the jars into the hot water and set timer for 3 hours.
- Once ready, cool and serve.

**Nutritional value.**

**Calories 175g**

**Carbs 38g**

**Protein.5.7g**

**Fat 0.8g**

# Chapter 2: Beef Recipes

## Beef With Greek Wraps.

**Servings 2.**

**Prep time. 20 minutes.**

**Cooking time.4 hours.**

**Ingredients.**

- 4 slices of red onion.
- 2 slices tomato.
- 2 tortilla wraps.
- 200g beef steak.
- Salt and pepper.
- 1 cup greekyogurt.
- 1 cucumber.
- 3tbsp olive oil.
- ½ lemon juiced.

**Directions.**

- Preheat the oven to 54C. Put steak and some olive oil in a zipper seal and set to cook for 4 hours.
- Mix cucumber, lemon, and yogurt and refrigerate. Sautemeat in a skillet till brown.
- Serve with toppings of tortilla, tomato, onion slices and yogurt dressing.

**Nutritional value.**

**Calories 356**

**Protein. 35**

**Carbs 12g**

**Fat 26g**

# Rib Eye Steak

**Servings 2**

**Prep time. 5 minutes.**

**Cooking time 4 hours.**

**Ingredients.**

- Seasoning.
- 200g rib eye steak.
- Salt.

**Directions.**

- Preheat the oven to 54C and immerse the steak to cook for 4 hours.
- Transfer and grill for 5 minutes.
- Serve hot.

**Nutritional value.**

**Calories 504.**

**Proteins 54g**

**Carbs 0g**

**Fats 30g**

# Corned Beef Served With Cabbage.

**Servings 2**

**Prep time 5 minutes.**

**Cooking time.2 days 50 minutes.**

**Ingredients.**

- 300g corned beef.
- 100g cabbage
- seasoning.

**Directions.**

- Preheat the oven, place the beef in a zip pouch and set to cook for 48 hours.
- Transfer beef to a pan and cook for some minutes. Add cabbage and cook till crispy as the beef dries up. Season and serve.

**Nutritional value.**

**Calories. 96**

**Protein 11g**

**Carbs 3g**

**Fat 2g**

# Beef Tenderloin In Green Beans.

**Servings 2.**

**Prep time. 30 minutes**

**Cooking time. 4 hours.**

**Ingredients.**

- 2 beef tenderloins.
- 100g green beans.
- Salt and pepper.
- 2 rosemary sprigs.
- 1tbsp butter.
- 1tbsp olive oil

**Directions.**

- Preheat the oven to 54C. Season the filets and add a sprig of rosemary then place in the oven for 4 hours. Add green beans in the last 30 minutes.
- Sauté in a skillet with butter to dry completely before serving.

**Nutritional value.**

**Calories. 504.**

**Proteins 54g**

**Fat 30g**

**Carbs 9g**

# Brisket.

**Servings .4**

**Prep time. 30 minutes.**

**Cooking time. 2 days.**

**Ingredients.**

- 500g brisket.
- 2 sprigs of parsley.
- 30g beef tallow.
- 1 clove of garlic.
- 1tbsp salt.
- 2tbsp butter.

**Directions.**

- Preheat the oven to 56C then season the brisket and add it to the pouch together with rosemary.
- Set to cook in the oven for 48 hours. Once ready, sauté in a skillet for 5 minutes and serve.

**Nutritional value.**

**Calories. 276**

**Protein 27g**

**Fat 12g**

**Carbs 0g**

# Steak Salad With Red Vinaigrette.

**Servings.3**

**Prep time 20 minutes.**

**Cooking time. 2 hours.**

**Ingredients.**

- 1 cup halved tomatoes.
- 300g flank steak.
- 1tbsp olive oil
- Salt and pepper.
- 1 head romaine.
- 2 pcs shallots.
- 2 blue cheese crumbles.
- 1 cup walnuts.

**Directions.**

- Preheat the oven to 55C. season the steak with salt, garlic powder and pepper then set to cook for 90 minutes.
- Once ready, transfer and slice appropriately.
- Set oven at 205C and toast the walnuts for sometime. Cut them into pieces the combine with the romaine, blue cheese, tomatoes, shallots, and steak.
- Place the cool walnuts on the salad and serve.

**Nutritional value.**

**Calories. 324**

**Protein 30g**

**carbs . 23g**

**Fat 26**

# Steak With Noodles.

**Servings 2**

**Prep time.5 minutes.**

**Cooking time.2 hours.**

**Ingredients.**

- 1 cup chicken stock
- 1 cup broccoli.
- 1 cup vegetable oil.
- 2 rib eye steaks.
- 2tbsp fish sauce.
- 1tbsp cornstarch
- 1 onion.

**Directions.**

- Preheat the oven to 57C and immerse steak for 1 hour.
- Deep fry the noodles separately and set aside.
- Fry onion in a skillet and add fish sauce, broccoli, corn starch and fish sauce. Combine the noodles and steak the and serve with the sauce.

**Nutritional value.**

**Calories. 367**

**Protein. 35g**

**Carbs. 28g**

**Fat.15g**

# Smoky Butter Steak.

**Servings. 2**

**Prep time. 5 minutes.**

**Cooking time 3 hours.**

**Ingredients.**

- 200g steak.
- Salt.
- Butter.
- Black pepper.

**Directions.**

- Preheat the oven to 57C and place the steak to cook for 3 hours.
- Mix salt, butter and pepper to form quenelles. Spare some butter.
- Once steak is ready, sauté in a hot skillet with butter to give it a juicy touch. Serve with quenelles

**Nutritional value.**

**Calories. 89**

**Protein. 8g**

**Carbs. 0g**

**Fats. 7g**

# Smoky Prime Rib.

**Servings 2**

**Prep time 5 minutes.**

**Cooking time. 24 hours.**

**Ingredients.**

- 500g rib steaks.
- Salt and pepper.
- 3tbsp butter.

**Directions.**

- Preheat the oven to 57C. Seal the steak and put into the water bath to cook for 24 hours.
- Once ready, sauté the ribs over butter in a skillet and serve.

**Nutritional value**

**Calories.134**

**Protein. 13g**

**Fat 7g**

**Carbs.0g**

# French Dip.

**Servings.2**

**Prep time. 30 minutes.**

**Cooking time. 2 hours.**

**Ingredients.**

- 100g ground steak
- 1 cup beef stock.
- Salt and pepper.
- 2 demi baguettes.
- 4 slices provolone cheese.

**Directions.**

- Preheat the oven to 60C and season the steak with salt. Put into a pouch and place in the water bath for 2 hours.
- Once done, slice the beef and heat through with the beef stock in a separate pan.
- Toast the rolls and top each of them with 2 slices of cheese and steak then serve.

**Nutritional value.**

**Calories.440**

**Protein.40g**

**Carbs.46g**

**fat.12g**

# Rubbed Beef Back Ribs

**Servings 2**

**Prep time.30 minutes.**

**Cooking time. 48 hours.**

**Ingredients.**

- 300g beef back ribs.
- 1tbsp paprika.
- 1tbsp garlic.
- 1tbsp mustard powder.
- 1tbsp paprika.
- 1tbsp ancho chili.
- 2tbsp thyme.
- Salt and pepper
- 1 cup brown sugar.

**Directions.**

- Preheat the oven to 450F. Season the ribs with salt and seal in a pouch and leave to cook for 48 hours.
- Whisk together all other ingredients and put aside. Once beef is ready. Toss the beef in the mixture and bake for 10 minutes till aromatic then serve.

**Nutritional value.**

**Calories 123**

**Protein 12g**

**Fats 7g**

**Carbs 2g**

# Beef Quesadilla.

**Servings.2**

**Prep time. 30 minutes**

**Cooking time 24 hours.**

**Ingredients.**

- 4 tortillas.
- 200g brisket beef.
- 2 carrots.
- 1 cup cheddar cheese.
- 2 garlic cloves.
- 1 bay leaf.
- 1 stalk celery
- 1 onion.
- Salt and pepper
- Olive oil.
- Butter
- 1tbsp sour cream
- Salsa.

**Directions.**

- Preheat the cooker to 85C and then combine brisket, carrot, salt and pepper, thyme, butter, garlic, and bay leaf in a zipper bag. Seal and set to cook for 24 hours.
- Transfer and shred the beef as you discard the vegetables.
- In a skillet, sauté the beef in cheese and top with tortillas then serve.

**Nutritional value**

**Calories.596**

**Proteins.31g**

**Carbs.37g**

**Fat.35g**

# Bone Marrow.

**Servings 2.**
**Prep time.15 minutes.**
**Cooking time. 1 hour**
**Ingredients.**

- 200g bones with marrow.
- Salt and pepper.
- 

**Directions**.

- Preheat the oven to 68C. Place the bones in pouches and set for 1 hour.
- Once ready,  broil the bones in a pan till golden brown and serve.

**Nutritional value.**
**Calories. 67**
**Proetin. 6g**
**Fat 5g**
**Carbs 0g**

# Pulled Beef Burgers.

**Servings.2**

**Prep time. 30 minutes.**

**Cooking time. 24 hours.**

**Ingredients.**

- 2 hamburger buns.
- 200g beef brisket.
- 2 slices red onion.
- 4 slices of tomato
- 2 slices cucumber.
- 2 carrots.
- Salt and pepper.
- 2tbsp olive oil.
- Bbq sauce.
- 1 clove garlic.
- 2 sprigs thyme.

**Directions.**

- Preheat the cooker to 85C. Put beef, carrot , thyme, bay leaf, garlic and butter in a zipper lock. Set to cook for 24 hours.
- When ready, shred beef and discard vegetables. Top with a mixture of the remaining ingredients and serve.

**Nutritional value.**

**Calories 456**

**Proteins.46g**

**Carbs.23g**

**Fat 30g.**

# Steak With Chimichurri Sauce.

**Servings. 2**

**Prep time.20 minutes**

**Cooking time.4 hours**

**Ingredients.**

- 1 cup chopped cilantro.
- 200g steak
- 1 cup chopped parsley.
- ½ cup olive oil.
- 1tbsp chile flakes.
- 3tbsp red wine vinegar.
- 1tbsp thaichile.

**Directions.**

- Preheat the oven to 54C
- Place the steak with some olive oil in two zip closes and set to cook for 4 hours.
- Combine the other items and grind them in a mortar. Once the steak is ready, sauté in a skillet with olive oil and serve with the chimichurri.

**Nutritional value.**

**Calories. 123**

**Carbs.5g**

**Protein 12g**

**Fats 10g**

# Potato And Steak Bites.

**Servings 2.**

**Prep time. 10 minutes**

**Cooking time. 4 hours**

**Ingredients.**

- 2tbsp butter.
- 1tbsp dijon mustard.
- 1 potato.
- 250g steak.
- 1 cucumber.
- 3 sprigs thyme.

**Directions.**

- Preheat the oven to 54C. Put the steak and some butter in a zip seal and set to cook for 4 hours.
- Boil the potato in a pot until tender. Fry in a skillet together with thyme till brown.
- For steak, heat butter and dijon mustard and saute the steak till brown.
- Combine and serve.

**Nutritional value.**

**Calories 245**

**Protein 24.**

**Carbs 19g**

**Fat 12g**

# Chapter 3: Fish And Seafood Recipes.

## Prawns With Singaporian Noodles.

**Servings 2**

**Prep time 15 minutes.**

**Cooking time. 45 minutes.**

**Ingredients.**

- 1tbsp soy
- 1tbsp curry powder.
- 200g prawns.
- 200g noodles.
- 1tbsp Chinese rice wine sauce.
- Vegetable oil.

**Directions.**

- Cook prawns in a water bath for 30 minutes.
- Heat oil in a pan and add soy sauce, curry powder and rice wine sauce. Add noodles and cook till well mixed with the sauce.
- Mix with prawns, garnish and serve.

**Nutritional value.**

**Calories 456**

**Proteins. 35g**

**Carbs 44g**

**Fat.12g**

# Lobster Rolls.

**Servings.2**

**Prep time. 15 minutes.**

**Cooking time. 1 hour.**

**Ingredients.**

- 2 lobster tails.
- 1tbsp butter.
- Salt and pepper.
- 1tbsp lemon juice.
- 1tbsp mayonnaise.

**Directions.**

- Preheat the water bath to 140F.
- Shell the tails and set to cook in the water bath for 25 minutes.
- Transfer and refrigerate for 30 minutes.
- Top with mayonnaise and lemon juice to serve.

**Nutritional value.**

**Calories. 290**

**Carbs 34g**

**Protein 24g**

**Fat 6g**

# Rosemary Lemon Salmon.

Servings 2

Prep time. 5 minutes.

Cooking time. 40 minutes.

Ingredients.

- 200g salmon.
- 1tbsp rosemary.
- 1tbsp garlic powder.
- Salt and pepper.
- 2 garlic cloves.
- Olive oil. 1tbsp lemon zest.
- 1tbsp lemon juice.

**Directions.**

- Preheat the cooker to 45C. Whisk together all ingredients except salmon until emulsified. Put the mixture and salmons into a zipper sealed bag and let cook for 30 minutes.
- Fry the garlic clove in a pan till brown and keep aside. Sauté the salmons in the same oil for 3 minutes.
- Garnish with garlic and capers then serve as desired.

**Nutritional value.**

**Calories 166**

**Protein 24g**

**Fat 6g**

**Carbs 0g**

# Salmon The Dutch Way.

**Servings 2**

**Prep time. 20 minutes.**

**Cooking time. 50 minutes.**

**Ingredients.**

- 2 salmons.
- 1 cup water.
- 1tbsp cayenne. Salt and pepper.
- 1 egg yolk.
- 1tbsp butter.
- 1 shallot.
- Lemon juice.

**Directions.**

- Preheat the cooker to 45C
- Salt the salmon and keep aside.
- Put the rest of the items into a sealable bag and set to cook for 30 minutes together with the salmon
- Sear the salmon in a skillet and blend the other mixture. Serve together.

**Nutritional value.**

**Calories 195**

**Protein 21g**

**Carbs 8g**

**Fat 15g**

# Braised Swordfish Steak.

**Servings 2.**

**Prep time. 10 minutes**

**Cooking time. 30 minutes.**

**Ingredients.**

- 1tbsp rice wine vinegar.
- 1tbsp brown sugar.
- 1tbsp sesame oil.
- Minced ginger
- 1tbsp soy sauce.
- 200g swordfish steak.

**Directions.**

- Combine the fish, minced ginger, sugar, red wine vinegar,sesame oil and tamari in a zipper seal bag. Set to cook for 30 minutes,
- Transfer in serving plates and top with the rest of the ingredients before serving.

**Nutritional value.**

**Calories 234**

**Protein, 25g**

**Carbs 2g**

**Fat 16g**

# Sous Vide Halibut.

**Servings 2.**

**Prep time. 10 minutes.**

**Cooking time. 45 minutes.**

**Ingredients.**

- 2 halibut fillets frozen.
- Salt and pepper.
- 2tbsp olive oil.
- Favorite aromatic spices.

**Directions.**

- Preheat the oven. Season the halibut with salt and butter then put in zip bags and seal. Set to cook for 45 minutes.
- Heat oil in a skillet and add the cooked halibut fillets. Add flavorings and sear for 3 minutes then serve.

**Nutritional value.**

**Calories.94**

**Proteins 17g**

**Fat 1g**

**Carbs 0g**

# Sous Vide Tuna.

**Servings 2.**

**Prep time 10 minutes.**

**Cooking time 45 minutes.**

**Ingredients.**

- 200g tuna steaks frozen.
- Salt and pepper.
- Olive oil.
- Favorite aromatics.
- 60g sesame seeds.

**Directions.**

- Preheat the oven to 54C. Put the tuna steaks in a zip sealed bag and set to cook for 45 minutes.
- Transfer fish and roll over seasonings and spices. Sear in a skillet with heated olive oil till brown on both sides.
- Slice and serve.

**Nutritional value.**

**Calories 87**

**Carbs 0g**

**Protein.10g**

**Fat 6g**

# Sous Vide Octopus.

**Servings. 2**

**Prep time. 20 minutes.**

**Cooking time. 8 hours.**

**Ingredients.**

- 1 octopus whole.
- 1 tbsp rosemary.
- 1 tbsp thyme.
- Olive oil.
- Juiced red cabbage.
- Salt and pepper.

**Directions.**

- Remove the entrails, eyes and beak and clean the octopus in running water.
- Put the octopus and the other ingredients in a sealable zip close bag and set to cook for 8 hours.
- Transfer and remove any loose skin parts. Sauté in a skillet and serve.

**Nutritional value**

**Calories 107.**

**Protein.9g**

**Carbs.6g**

**Fat.4g**

# Prawn Cocktail Salad.

**Servings 2.**

**Prep time 15 minutes.**

**Cooking time. 15 minutes.**

**Ingredients.**

- 20 small prawns.
- Chopped romaine lettuce.
- 1 avocado.
- Salt and pepper.
- Tomatoes.
- 2 scallions.
- 1tbsp lemon juice
- 1tbsp ketchup
- 1tbsp mayonnaise.

**Directions.**

- Preheat oven to 54C and cook prawns in a sealed zip bag for 15 minutes.
- Mix together all vegetables to make the salad. Seer the prawns in hot oil over a skillet.
- Serve as desired.

**Nutritional value.**

**Calories. 210**

**Carbs . 16g**

**Protein .20g**

**Fat.4g**

# Prawn Pasta Salad.

**Servings.2**

**Prep time.20 minutes.**

**Cooking time. 20 minutes.**

**Ingredients.**

- 1 cup spinach.
- 2 tomatoes.
- 20 small prawns.
- 21 cup pasta.
- 1tbsp dijon mustard.
- Salt and pepper.
- 1tbsp olive oil.
- 1tbsp lemon juice.
- 1green onion.

**Directions.**

- Preheat the bath to 65C. Seal the prawns in a zip seal bag and cook for 20 minutes.
- Mix all the vegetables and sear the prawns in a skillet. Mix and serve.

**Nutritional value.**

**Calories. 356**

**Proteins 26g**

**Carbs 15g**

**Fat 5g**

# Fish Served With Xo Sauce.

**Servings 2.**

**Prep time. 10 minutes**

**Cooking time. 40 minutes.**

**Ingredients.**

- 200g fish fillets.
- 1tbsp xo sauce.
- 1tbsp soy sauce.
- 1tbsp ginger
- 1 onion.
- Salt and pepper.
- 1tbsp olive oil.

**Directions.**

- Preheat the oven to 65C and cook the fillets for 30 minutes in the water bath.
- Heat oil in a pan and fry cook ginger, xo and soy sauces.
- Serve the mixture with fillets.

**Nutritional value.**

**Calories. 145**

**Carbs. 2g**

**Fat. 6g**

**Protein 15g.**

# Chapter 4: Pork Recipes.

## Salsa Verde Pork

**Servings. 2**

**Prep time. 30 minutes**

**Cooking time. 18 hours.**

**Ingredients.**

- 3 tomatillos.
- 250g pork shoulders
- Vegetable oil.
- Salt and pepper.
- 2 sprigs thyme.
- ¼ cup cilantro.
- 2 bay leaves.
- 1 jalapeno.

**Directions.**

- Season pork with salt, thyme, garlic and bay leaves. Put in a zipper seal bag and cook for 18 hours at 71C.
- Blend tomatillo and jalapeno. Once pork is ready, shred and serve with salsa verde.

**Nutritional value.**

**Calories. 154**

**Proteins 23g**

**Fats 6g**

**Carbs. 0g**

# Deep Fried Pork.

**Servings 2**

**Prep time. 1hour**

**Cooking time 24 hours.**

**Ingredients.**

- 250g pork belly
- 1 clove garlic
- 1 green onion
- Salt and pepper.
- Olive oil.
- 1tbsp thaichillies.
- Ginger.

**Directions.**

- Seal the pork with onion, pepper and garlic in a zip close bag and cook for 24 hours at 68C.
- Separate the pork and the cooking liquid. Cut pork into cubes and attach to bamboo skewers. Fry garlic and Thaichilies in a sauce pan. Add the cooking liquid to make a thick sauce. Sprinkle the sauce over pork and serve.

**Nutritional value.**

**Calories. 120**

**Proteins 23g**

**Carbs. 0g**

**fat . 6g**

# Babi Chin.

**Servings. 2**

**Prep time 10 minutes.**

**Cooking time. 7 hours.**

**Ingredients.**

- 250g pork
- 2 shitake
- 2 cloves garlic
- 1tbsp sugar
- Salt and pepper.
- Coriander
- 2tbsp honey.
- 2 shallots
- 2-star anise.
- Olive oil.

**Directions.**

- Combine all the ingredients in a sealed bag and cook for 7 hours at 80C.
- Separate the pork from the rest.
- Fry the vegetables in a saucepan to make a thick sauce. Combine with pork and serve.

**Nutritional value.**

**Calories. 156**

**Proteins. 25g**

**Carbs 16g**

**fats . 8g**

# Canadian Bacon

**Servings 2**

**Prep time. 10 minutes.**

**Cooking time. 12 hours**

**Ingredients.**

- 250g bacon
- 3tbsp canola oil.

**Directions.**

- Seal the bacon in a zip bag and cook in the water bath for 12 hours at 62C.
- Broil the bacon in a pan with canola oil till brown then serve.

**Nutritional value.**

**Calories. 167**

**Protein. 15g**

**Fat 16g**

**Carbs 0g**

# Sous Vide Bacon.

**Servings 2**

**Prep time. 20 minutes**

**Cooking time. 12 hours.**

**Ingredients.**

- 250g bacon.

**Directions.**

- Seal pork well and cook for 12 hours at 68C.
- Slice the pork and broil in a skillet till brown, serve.

**Nutritional value.**

**Calories. 98**

**Carbs. 0**

**Fat 10g**

**Proteins 8g.**

# Pork Tenderloin.

**Servings 2**

**Prep time. 10 minutes.**

**Cooking time.  1 hour.**

**Ingredients.**

- 200g pork tenderloins.
- 2tbsp canola oil.
- Fresh herbs
- Salt and pepper.
- Aromatics
- 15g butter.

**Directions.**

- Salt the pork and seal with herbs and aromatics. Cook for 1 hour.
- Slice and roll over black pepper.  Broil for 5 minutes in oil till brown.
- serve.

**Nutritional value.**

**Calories. 185**

**Protein. 31g**

**Carbs 0g**

**Fat 25g**

# Pork Chops.

**Servings 2**

**Prep time. 15 minutes.**

**Cooking time. 1 hour.**

**Ingredients.**

- 250g pork sliced
- Salt and pepper
- Favorite aromatics.
- 15g butter.

**Directions.**

- Seal the pork with aromatics and herbs and cook in a waterbath for 1 hour. Once done, discard the aromatics and dry the pork.
- Heat butter and canola oil in a skillet and broil pork till brown. Sear with the sauce and serve.

**Nutritional value**

**Calories 120**

**Proteins 12**

**Carbs 2.1g**

**Fat 14g**

# Chapter 5: Cocktails And Beverages.

## Infused Bacon.

**Servings 2**

**Prep time. 20 minutes.**

**Cooking time. 5 hours.**

**Ingredients.**

- 3tbsp bacon grease.
- 500ml vodka.
- 250g bacon.

**Directions.**

- Bake the bacon for 15 minutes at 68C.
- Put all the ingredients in a seal bag and set in the bath for 45 minutes. Strain the liquid and refrigerate for 3 hours.
- Skim fat and serve.

**Nutritional value.**

**Calories 45**

**Protein 5g**

**Carbs 0g**

**Fat. 3g**

# Spiced Rum.

**Servings 2**

**Prep time. 20 minutes**

**Cooking time. 2 hours**

**Ingredients.**

- 500ml rum
- Orange zest.
- 1 star anise.
- 1 whole clove
- 1 vanilla beans
- 1 cinnamon stick.
- 2 peppercorns

**Directions.**

- Put all the ingredients in a sealable bag and put in the water bath for 2 hours at 67C.
- Strain the ingredients and refrigerate before serving.

**Nutritional value.**

**Calories 69**

**Proteins 0g**

**Fats0g**

**Carbs.0g**

# Mulled Wine.

**Servings 2**

**Prep time 15 minutes.**

**Cooking time. 1 hour.**

**Ingredients.**

- 2 oranges juiced
- 1-star anise.
- 1 bottle red wine
- Bay leaf
- 1 cinnamon stick
- 1 vanilla pod
- 50g caster sugar.

**Directions.**

- Combine all ingredients and put into two zip-close bags. Set in a waterbath for 1 hour and refrigerate before serving,

**Nutritional value.**

**Calories. 106**

**Fat. 0.26g**

**Protein. 0.51g**

**Carbs. 18g**

# Chilli Vodka.

**Servings 2**

**Prep time. 5 minutes**

**Cooking time 2 hours.**

**Ingredients.**

- 1 bottle vodka
- 3 chilies.

**Directions.**

- Put the chilies and pour the vodka in a sealable bag. Set in the water bath for 2 hours.
- Strain and serve as desired.

**Nutritional value.**

**Calories. 64**

**Fat.0g**

**Protein. 0g**

**Carbs. 0g**

# Hot Spiced Cider.

**Servings 2**

**Prep time. 5 minutes**

**Cooking time. 1 hour.**

**Ingredients.**

- 500ml apple cider.
- Orange juice.
- 1 cinnamon stick.
- Maple syrup
- 1tbsp peppercorns.

**Directions.**

- Put all the ingredients in a sealable bag and set in the water bath for 1 hour at 60C.
- Strain and serve.

**Nutritional value.**

**Calories 80**

**Protein 0g**

**Fats 0g**

**Carbs 20g**

# Mint Julep.

**Servings 6**

**Prep time 10 minutes.**

**Cooking time. 2 hours**

**Ingredients.**

- 2 cups water
- 2 cups fresh mint
- 2 cups sugar
- 1 cup bourbon

**Directions.**

- Put all ingredients in a sealable bag and set in the water bath for 2 hours.
- Refrigerate and serve.

**Nutritional value**

**Calories 126**

**Proteins 0g**

**Carbs 2.61g**

**Fats. 0g**

# Lemon Thyme Syrup.

**Servings 2**

**Prep time. 10 minutes.**

**Cooking time. 2 hours.**

**Ingredients.**

- 2 bunches thyme
- 1 cup water
- 1 cup sugar
- 2 lemons sliced.

**Directions.**

- Put the ingredients in a zip seal bag and set to cook for 2 hours.
- Strain and refrigerate before serving.

**Nutritional value.**

**Calories 54**

**Protein. 0g**

**Fats .0g**

**Carbs. 25g**

# Lavender Syrup.

**Servings 4**

**Prep time 5 minutes.**

**Cooking time. 1 hour.**

**Ingredients.**

- 1 cup sugar
- 1 cup water
- 10ml lavender dried.

**Directions.**

- Put all ingredients in a zip seal bag and place in the water bath for 1 hour at 67C.
- Strain and refrigerate.

**Nutritional value**

**Calories. 90**

**Protein. 0g**

**Carbs.23g**

**Fat.0g**

# Chapter 6: Sauces and condiments.

## Garlic Confit.

**Servings. 2**

**Prep time. 15 minutes.**

**Cooking time. 4 hours**

**Ingredients.**

- 200g garlic cloves
- Kosher salt
- 1tbsp olive oil.

**Directions.**

- Combine ingredients in a zipper bag and set to cook for 4 hours in a waterbath at 78C.
- Refrigerate and serve.

**Nutritional value.**

**Calories. 68**

**Carbs. 2g**

**Protein 3g**

**Fat. 0.98g**

# Orange Thyme- Maple Syrup.

**Servings 2**

**prep time. 15 minutes**

**Cooking time. 1 hour.**

**Ingredients.**

- 100g maple syrup
- Fresh thyme.
- A pinch of salt.
- 2tbsp orange zest.

**Directions.**

- Combine all ingredients in a large zipper bag and set in the water bath for 1 hour.
- Strain and serve.

**Nutritional value.**

**Calories 89**

**Proteins. 2**

**Fat. 3g**

**Carbs 6g**

# Blueberry Maple Syrup.

**Servings 2**

**Prep time. 15 minutes.**

**Cooking time. 1 hour**

**Ingredients.**

- Maple syrup
- 250g blueberries.
- Lemon zest.
- Sea salt.
- Lemon juice.

**Directions.**

- Combine all ingredients in a sealed bag and set to cook in the water bath for 1 hour at 79C.
- Transfer and refrigerate.

**Nutritional value.**

**Calories. 160**

**Protein.2.5g**

**Fat.0g**

**Carbs. 41g**

# Strawberry Basil Syrup.

**Servings 2**

**Prep time. 15 minutes.**

**Cooking time. 1 hour.**

**Ingredients.**

- Maple syrup.
- 200g strawberries.
- 100g basil leaves.
- Sea salt.

**Directions.**

- Combine the ingredients in a seal and set in the water bath at 57C for 1 hour.
- Remove basil and refrigerate.

**Nutritional value.**

**Calories. 67**

**Protein 0g**

**Carbs 12g**

**Fat 0g.**

# Ancho Chile Oil.

**Servings 2**

**Prep time. 15 minutes.**

**Cooking time. 1 hour**

**Ingredients.**

- 1 dried ancho chile.
- Kosher salt.
- Canola oil.
- 2 garlic cloves.
- Red wine vinegar.

**Directions.**

- Put all ingredients in a seal bag and set in the water bath for 1 hour at 79C.
- Refrigerate.

**Nutritional value.**

**Calories. 120**

**Carbs.0g**

**Protein. 0g**

**Fat. 14g**

# Sauce Hollandaise.

**Servings 2**

**Prep time. 20 minutes**

**Cooking time. 30 minutes.**

**Ingredients.**

- 2 egg yolks
- White wine sauce.
- 1tbsp champagne vinegar.
- 1 shallot.
- 1tbsp lemon juice
- Butter.
- thyme.

## Directions.

- Boil wine, thyme, shallots and vinegar in a saucepan for 10 minutes. Strain and add eggs and for 3 seconds.
- Seal in a bag and set in the water bath for 30 minutes and serve.

## Nutritional value.

## Calories.62

## Protein. 3g

## Carbs. 2g

## Fat.0.86g

# Dulce De Leche.

**Servings 2**

**Prep time. 5 minutes.**

**Cooking time. 12 hours.**

**Ingredients.**

- 500ml sweetened milk.

**Directions.**

- Put the milk in a canning jar and set in the water bath for 12 hours.
- Remove and serve.

**Nutritional value.**

**Calories. 122**

**Protein 8g**

**Carbs 12**

**Fats 4.8g**

# Mezcal Cream.

**Servings 2**

**Prep time. 15 minutes**

**Cooking time. 30 minutes.**

**Ingredients.**

- ½ cup heavy cream.
- ½ cup mezcal.
- ½ cup ultrafine sugar.
- 2 egg yolks.
- Salt
- Vanilla.

**Directions.**

- Blend all the ingredients for 2 minutes. Transfer and set in a water bath for 30 minutes at 180F.
- Serve and refrigerate.

**Nutritional value.**

**Calories. 130**

**Fat. 10.12g**

**Carbs. 3g**

**Proteins. 6g**

# Crème Fraiche.

**Servings. 2**

**Prep time.**

**Cooking time. 12 hours.**

**Ingredients.**

- 1 cup heavy cream
- 6tbsp buttermilk.

**Directions.**

- Mix ingredients in a canning jar and set in a water bath for 12 hours at 40C.
- Refrigerate and serve.

**Nutritional value.**

**Calories. 110**

**Protein. 0g**

**Carbs.0g**

**Fat. 11g**

# English Vanilla

**Servings 2**

**Prep time.15 minutes.**

**Cooking time 1 hour**

**Ingredients.**

- 1 cup milk
- 1 cup heavy cream
- Kosher salt
- 1tbsp fine sugar.
- 1tbsp vanilla bean paste.
- 2 egg yolks.

**Directions.**

- Blend all ingredients for 1 minute and put in a canning jar. Set in a water bath for 1 hour
- Refrigerate and serve.

**Nutritional value.**

**Calories. 213**

**Protein. 20g**

**Fat. 19g**

**Carbs.2.6g**

# Shallot Confit.

**Servings 2**

**Prep time. 10 minutes.**

**Cooking time. 2 hours.**

**Ingredients.**

- 2 shallots
- 50g granulated sugar.
- Kosher salt.
- Olive oil.

**Directions.**

- Seal the ingredients well and set in a waterbath for 2 hours at 87C. Transfer and refrigerate.

**Nutritional value.**

**Calories. 15**

**Fat.1g**

**Proteins.2g**

**Carbs.8g**

# Chapter 7: Desserts

## Chocolate Cake.

**Servings 2**

**Prep time. 10 minutes**

**Cooking time. 1 hour.**

**Ingredients.**

- 2 eggs
- 100g chocolate
- Butter.

**Directions.**

- Mix the chocolate and butter and put in the oven for 5 minutes.
- Add eggs and whisk together. put batter in a jar and set in water bath for 1 hour
- Cool before serving.

**Nutritional value.**

**Calories. 235**

**Protein. 9g**

**Carbs.34g**

**Fat. 12g**

# Lemon Cheese Cake.

**Servings 2**

**Prep time. 15 minutes**

**Cooking time. 2 hours.**

**Ingredients.**

- 200g cheese cream
- 2 eggs.
- 1tbsp butter
- 1tbsp lemon juice.
- 1tbsp vanilla extract.
- 1tbsp salt
- Lemon rind ground.

**Directions.**

- Make batter by mixing the ingredients. Put in two jars and close.
- Set to bake in a water bath at 174C. Cool before serving.

**Nutritional value.**

**Calories. 340**

**Carbs 34g**

**Fat 28g**

**Protein. 5g**

# Blueberry Clafoutis.

**Servings 2**

**Prep time. 5 minutes.**

**Cooking time.  1 hour.**

**Ingredients.**

- Cake mix.
- 3 blueberries.

**Directions.**

- Put the mix in 2 canning jars and top with a blueberry each.
- Set to cook for 1 hour at 85C.
- Cool before serving.

**Nutritional value.**

**Calories.267**

**Protein. 20g**

**Carbs. 27g**

**Fat. 9g**

# Chocolate Steam Boat Cake.

**Servings 2**

**Prep time. 5 minutes.**

**Cooking time. 1 hour**

**Ingredients.**

- Cake mix.
- 50g cocoa powder.

**Directions.**

- Whisk together the ingredients till smooth.
- Put in a closed jar and set in the water bath for 1 hour.
- Cool and slice to serve.

**Nutritional value.**

**Calories 154**

**Protein 9g**

**Carbs 16g**

**Fat.13g**

# Cinnamon Almond Cake.

**Servings. 2**

**Prep time 5 minutes**

**Cooking time 2 hours**

**Ingredients.**

- Cinnamon cake mix
- 50g almonds.

**Directions.**

- Whisk together all ingredients and pour into 2 jars. Close and set in the water bath for 2 hours.
- Cool before serving.

**Nutritional value.**

**Calories 167**

**Carbs 17g**

**Fat.7g**

**Protein 10g**

# Strawberries With Chocolate.

**Servings 2.**

**Prep time. 5 minutes.**

**Cooking time. 20 minutes.**

**Ingredients.**

- 200g chocolate chips.
- 1tbsp cayenne strawberries
- 1tbsp cinnamon.

**Directions.**

- Place chocolate and cinnamon in the water bath for 10 minutes until. Remove and dip the strawberries in the mixture. Refrigerate and serve.

**Nutritional value**

**Calories 120**

**Carbs.22g**

**Fat. 3g**

**Protein. 2g**

# Flavoredcrème Brulee.

**Servings 2**

**Prep time 15 minutes**

**Cooking time 45 minutes.**

**Ingredients.**

- 200ml whipping cream
- 50g granulated sugar.

- 2 egg yolks.
- 1tbsp vanilla extract.
- Favorite flavorings.

## Directions.

- Mix eggs and sugar till pale. Heat the sour cream in a pan aside.
- Mix with cream and whisk. put in jars and close. Set in bath for 45 minutes. Refrigerate and serve.

## Nutritional value.

**calories 90**

**Carbs .8g**

**Fat3g**

**Protein 4g**

# Chapter 8: Fruit Recipes.

## Mango.

**Servings 2.**

**Prep time. 15 minutes.**

**Cooking time. 20 minutes.**

**Ingredients**

- 1 mango
- 1 cup coconut milk.
- Sugar
- Ginger.
- Lemon grass.
- 1 red chili.

**Directions.**

- Slice the mango and separate seed from flesh.
- Heat the rest of the ingredients in a pan to form syrup. Add everything in a jar and seal. Set in the water bath for 20 minutes. Chill and serve.

**Nutritional value.**

**Calories. 98**

**Carbs. 11g**

**Fat 6g**

**Protein. 4g**

# Apricots.

**Servings 2**

**Prep time 10 minutes.**

**Cooking time. 20 minutes.**

**Ingredients.**

- 50ml water
- 2 apricots.
- 50ml sugar.

**Directions.**

- Boil sugar and water in a bag to make a syrup.
- Halve the apricots and remove stones. Pour the syrup into the halves and seal. Set in the water bath for 40 minutes
- Transfer and serve.

**Nutritional value**

**Calories. 17**

**Carbs. 3g**

**Protein. 0.9g**

**Fat.0.13**

# Pears.

**Servings 2**

**Prep time 10 minutes**

**Cooking time. 30 minutes.**

**Ingredients.**

- 2 pears skinned and halved.
- 1 vanilla bean pod.
- 100g sugar syrup.

**Directions.**

- Put the pears and the sugar syrup in a bag and seal. Set for 30 minutes.
- Drain the excess liquid and serve.

**Nutritional value.**

**Calories.  96**

**Protein. 0.63g**

**Carbs. 25g**

**Fat. 0.23g**

# Macerated Ctrawberries.

**Servings 2**

**Prep time. 10 minutes.**

**Cooking time. 2 days.**

**Ingredients.**

- 250g strawberries.
- 50ml white sweet wine.

**Directions.**

- Put strawberries in a jar and pour wine over them.
- Use immediately or refrigerate.

**Nutritional value**

**Calories 48**

**Carbs 11g**

**Proteins 3g**

**Fat 1.2g**

# Plums.

**Servings 2**

**Prep time 10 minutes.**

**Cooking time. 20 minutes.**

**Ingredients.**

- 2 plums
- 50g castor sugar.

**Directions.**

- Put the plums in a bag and set in the water bath for 20 minutes.
- Sprinkle sugar and serve.

**Nutritional value.**

**Calories. 30**

**carbs 7g**

**Protein. 0.46g**

**Fat. 0.23g**

# Sous Vide Pineapples.

**Servings 2**

**Prep time. 10 minutes.**

**Cooking time. 8 hours.**

**Ingredients.**

- ½ a pineapple
- 50g brown sugar.

**Directions.**

- Skin the pineapples remove the hard flesh. Roll the pineapples in sugar and set in the water bath for 8 hours at 80C.
- Serve chilled.

**Nutritional value.**

**Calories. 78**

**Carbs 20.38g**

**Protein 0.87g**

**Carbs. 0.05g**

# Damsons

**Servings 2.**

**Prep time. 40 minutes.**

**Cook time. 40 minutes.**

**Ingredients.**

- 200g damsons.
- 50g sugar 1 cup water.

**Directions.**

- Half the damsons and put them into a bag. Heat sugar and water till sugar is dissolved and add the syrup into the bag.
- Seal and set at the water bath for 40 minutes at 70C.
- Transfer and serve.

**Nutritional value.**

**Calories. 78**

**Proteins. 2g**

**Carbs 12g**

**Fat. 5g**

# Yummy Toffee Apple.

**Servings 2**

**Prep 1 hour.**

**Cooking time 5 hours.**

**Ingredients.**

- 2 apples.
- 100g brown sugar.
- 50ml honey.
- 200ml white wine sauce.

**Directions.**

- Heat sugar, honey and sauce to form caramel. Cool aside.
- Peel apples and mix the with the caramel. Seal them and set in the cooker for 5 hours. Cool and serve.

**Nutritional value.**

**Calories. 67**

**Carbs 8g**

**Protein 0.76g**

**Fat. 2g**

# Chapter 9: Lamb Recipes.

## Garam Gasala Lamb Racks.

**Servings 2.**

**Prep time. 10 minutes**

**Cooking time. 2 hours.**

**Ingredients.**

- 300g baby lamb pork.
- Garam masala.
- Salt and pepper.

**Directions.**

- Season lamb with salt and pepper and roll over garam masala. Put in a bag and seal. Set in a water bath for 2 hours at 57C.
- Pat dry and sear in a skillet.
- Slice and serve.

**Nutritional value**

**Calories 248**

**Carbs 0g**

**Fat 18g**

**Protein 20g**

# Lamb Loin Chops.

**Servings 2**

**Prep time. 10 minutes.**

**Cooking time. 3 hours.**

**Ingredients.**

- 4 lamb loins
- 8 sprigs rosemary
- 8 sprigs of thyme.
- 2 garlic cloves.
- Salt and pepper.

**Directions.**

- Put the ingredients in a bag and seal. Set for 3 hours at 131F.
- Sear the lab and herbs in a skillet till brown. Slice and serve.

**Nutritional value.**

**Calories 234**

**Proteins 24**

**Fats 19g**

**Carbs 0g**

# Seasoned Lamb Steaks.

**Servings. 2**

**Prep time 4 hours.**

**Cooking time 6 hours.**

**Ingredients.**

- 250g lamb legs.
- 150ml olive oil.
- 2 sprigs rosemary.
- 2 sprigs thyme
- 2 cloves garlic.
- Sat and pepper.
- 1 bay leaf.

**Directions.**

- Heat thyme, rosemary, garlic and bay leaf in the olive oil in a pan to make the marinade.
- Salt the lamb steaks and put them in a bag. Set for 6 hours in the cooker at 56C.
- Sear the steak in a skillet till brown and serve.

**Nutritional value**

**Calories 250**

**Protein 26g**

**Carbs 0g**

**Fat 19g**

# Seasoned Lamb Loins.

**Servings 2**

**Prep time 10 minutes.**

**Cooking time. 2 hours.**

**Ingredients.**

- 250g lamb loins
- 2tbsp honey
- Salt and pepper.
- 50g mild mustard.
- 1tbsp basil
- Lemon zest.
- Garlic.

**Directions.**

- Sear the lamb in olive oil till brown. Put in a bag and seal. Set in the water bath for 2 hours at 60C
- Mix the rest of the ingredients in a bowl. Spread the mixture on the lamb and broil for 5 minutes then serve.

**Nutritional value.**

**Calories 256**

**Protein 27g**

**Carbs 0g**

**Fat 23g**

# Rump Of Lamb.

**Servings 2**

**Prep time 30 minutes**

**Cooking time 50 minutes.**

**Ingredients.**

- 2 lamb rumps
- 50g tomato puree
- Salt and pepper.
- Olive puree
- 1 sprig rosemary.

**Directions.**

- Remove fat from the rumps. Salt the rumps and rub in tomato and olive purees.
- Seal and set in the water bath for 50 minutes. Remove and sear the lamb loin both sides till brown in a skillet.
- Serve.

**Nutritional value.**

**Calories. 208**

**Fat 15g**

**Protein 21g**

**Carbs. 5g**

# Lamb Neck Fillets

**Servings 2**

**Prep time. 1 hour**

**cooking time. 24 hours.**

**Ingredients.**

- 250g lamb neck fillets
- 1tbsp basil
- Salt and pepper
- 2 mint leaves.

**Directions.**

- Cut any sinews from the fillets. Cover each fillet with basil and mint leaves and season with salt.
- Put each in a bag and seal. Set in the bath for 24 hours at 55C.
- Sear in a pan till brown and serve

**Nutritional value.**

**Calories. 265**

**Protein. 24g**

**Fat 18g**

**Carbs 2g**

# Chapter 10: Game Recipes.

## Rabbit Legs.

**Servings 2**

**Prep time 20 minutes**

**Cooking time. 4 hours.**

**Ingredients.**

- 2 rabbit legs
- Kosher salt.
- Black pepper.
- 2 sprigs rosemary.
- Olive oil.

**Directions.**

- Season rabbit legs with salt and pepper then seal in a bag. Set for 3 hours in the bath at 60C.
- Once done, broil for 5 minutes till brown.

**Nutritional value**

**Calories.40**

**Proteins 5g**

**Fat 2g**

**Carbs 0g**

# Curried Goat Stew.

**Servings 2.**

**Prep time.30 minutes**

**Cooking time 24 hours.**

**Ingredients.**

- 250g goat meat.
- 2tbsp ginger
- 2tbsp cumin'
- 2tbsp paprika
- 1 clove garlic'
- 2tbsp olive oil
- 2tbsp salt and pepper
- 1 red pepper.
- 1 onion
- 2 tomatoes
- Curry powder.

**Directions.**

- Combine all the ingredients in a bag and seal. Set for 24 hours at 50C.
- Shred the meat and discard the bones. Return to the stew. Garnish and serve.

**Nutritional value.**

**Calories. 122**

**Proteins 22g**

**Fat 3g**

**Carbs 0g**

# Kangaroo Steak.

**Servings 2**

**Prep time 15 minutes**

**Cooking time 2 hours.**

**Ingredients.**

- 200g kangaroo steak
- 1 tbsp. olive oil
- Salt and pepper.
- 2tbsp wine.
- 1 clove garlic

**Directions.**

- Season kangaroo steak with salt and some olive oil. Seal in a bag with wine and garlic.
- Set for 2 hours at 67C in the bath. Once ready, sear the meat in a skillet till brown and serve.

**Nutritional value.**

**Calories 156**

**Protein 17g**

**Fat 10g**

**Carbs 4g**

# Quail Legs.

**Servings. 2**

**Prep time. 15 minutes.**

**Cooking time. 2 hours.**

**Ingredients.**

- 250g quail legs
- Salt and pepper.
- 2tbsp olive oil.

**Directions.**

- Salt the quail legs and seal in a pouch. Set for 3 hours in the bath at 76C.
- Sear the legs in a pan with olive oil till brown and serve.

**Nutritional value.**

**Calories 156**

**Protein 17g**

**Fat 13g**

**Carbs 2g**

# Quail Breast.

**Servings 2**

**Prep time 10 minutes**

**Cooking time 2 hours.**

**Ingredients.**

- Salt and pepper
- 2tbsp olive oil.
- 200g quail breast.

**Directions.**

- Salt the breasts and set in the bath for 2 hours.
- Sear the breasts in a skillet with olive oil till brown and serve.

**Nutritional value.**

**Calories 156**

**Protein 17g**

**Fat 12g**

**Carbs 2g**

# Chapter 11: Poultry Recipes

## Chicken Adobo.

**Servings. 2**

**Prep time 15 minutes.**

**Cooking time.4 hours.**

**Ingredients.**

- 250g chicken thighs
- Olive oil
- Salt and pepper.
- Soy sauce
- Honey.
- 2tbsp vinegar
- 2 cloves.

**Directions.**

- Salt the chicken thighs and put in a pouch with the other ingredients. Set for 4 hours at 67C.
- Shred the thighs and serve with the liquid.

**Nutritional value.**

**Calories. 134**

**Proteins 15g**

**Carbs 3g**

**Fat 8g**

# Crispy Chicken Wings.

## Servings 2

## Prep time 4 minutes

## Cooking time 2 hours

## Ingredients.

- 4 chicken wings.
- Salt and pepper.
- Olive oil
- 2tbsp cornstarch.
- 1 tbsp. pepper.

## Directions

- Salt the chicken wings and set in the bath for 2 hours. Once ready, pat dry. roll the wings on cornstarch and broil in a pan with olive oil till brown.
- Serve.

## Nutritional value

## Calories. 134

## Proteins 13g

## Carbs 4g

## Fat 5g

# No-Sear Chicken Breast.

**Servings 2**

**Prep time 5 minutes.**

**Cooking time. 1 hour.**

**Ingredients.**

- Boneless chicken breast
- Pepper
- Salt.
- Garlic powder.

**Directions.**

- Season the breasts and seal in a bag. drop in the bath for 2 hours and pat dry.
- Serve

**Nutritional value.**

**Calories 164**

**Proteins. 24g**

**Fat 13g**

**Carbs 0g**

# Ginger Marmalade Chicken.

**Servings 2**

**Prep time. 40 minutes**

**Cooking time. 4 hours**

**Ingredients.**

- 2tbsp marmalade.
- 250g chicken with skin and bones.
- Ginger.
- Salt and pepper.

**Directions.**

- Put all the ingredients in a bag and seal. Set for 4 hours inthe water bath.
- Broil the chicken at 260C for 5 minutes till the skin turns brown. serve.

**Nutritional value.**

**Calories. 245**

**Protein 27g**

**Carbs 0g**

**Fat. 23g**

# Duck Breast.

**Servings 1**

**Prep time 10 minutes**

**Cooking time. 2 hours.**

**Ingredients.**

- 2 duck breasts
- 2 sprigs thyme.
- Olive oil

**Directions.**

- Seal the duck breasts in a pouch and set for 2 hours at 70C.
- Sear the chicken in a skillet and serve.

**Nutritional value.**

**Calories. 67**

**Protein 8**

**Carbs 0**

**Fat 3g**

# Chicken Salad.

**Servings 2**

**Prep time 20 minutes.**

**Cooking time. 1 hour.**

**Ingredients.**

- 200g chicken steak
- Favorite vegetables
- Favorite spices.
- Olive oil
- Salt and pepper.

**Directions.**

- Coat the chicken with spices and set in the bath for 1 hour in a pouch,
- Toss the vegetables for salad. Sear the chicken and serve together.

**Nutritional value.**

**Calories 256**

**Carbs 14g**

**Fat 12g**

**Protein 27g**

# Buffalo Ranch Chicken.

**Servings 4**

**Prep time. 20 minutes**

**Cooking time. 45 minutes.**

**Ingredients.**

- 200g chicken thighs.
- 1pkt ranch dip.
- 1 cup sauce.
- 1tbsp butter.
- 20g cheddar cheese.
- 20g cream cheese.

**Instructions.**

- Put all ingredients in a bag and seal. Set in the water bath for 45 minutes.
- Sear the chicken in a broiler and serve hot

**Nutritional value.**

**Calories. 341**

**Proteins.42g**

**Fat.23.71g**

**Carbs. 9.98g**

# Chicken Satay.

**Prep time. 5 minutes**

**Cooking time. 1 hour**

**Ingredients.**

- 200g chicken steak
- Satay sauce.

**Directions.**

- Seal chicken and set in the bath for 1 hour. Attach meat to skewers and sear.
- Serve.

**Nutritional value.**

**Calories 123**

**Protein 15g**

**Carbs 0g**

**Fat 9g**

# Chapter 12: Soups And Stew Recipes

## Minestrone Soup.

**Servings 4**

**Prep time 30 minutes.**

**Cooking time 3 hours.**

**Ingredients.**

- 200g elbow pasta.
- 100g bone broth.
- 100g cannellini beans.
- ½ cup spinach.
- 2 tomatoes.
- I onion
- 1 carrot.
- Favorite spices.
- Olive oil.

**Directions.**

- Put all ingredients except onion and olive oil in a bag and seal. Set in the water bath for 3 hours at 76C.
- Fry onion in a skillet and add the mix. Cook for 5 minutes, garnish and serve.

**Nutritional value.**

**Calories 186**

**Fats.4.59g**

**Protein.10.12**

**Carbs.26.34g**

# Chicken Stock.

**Servings. 3**

**Prep time. 10 minutes.**

**Cooking time. 2 hours.**

**Ingredients.**

- 200g bone-in chicken.
- 1 onion.
- 2 celery sticks.
- 1 carrot.
- Salt.
- Olive oil.

**Directions.**

- Put all the ingredients in the pouch and set in the water bath for 2 hours .
- Transfer and strain. Put in jars .
- Serve or refrigerate.
- Nutritional value.

**Calories. 12**

**Fat. 0.29g**

**Carbs. 1.51g**

**Protein.0.95g.**

# Carrot And Zucchini Soup.

**Servings 2.**

**Prep time. 35 minutes.**

**Cooking time.5 hours.**

**Ingredients.**

- 3 zucchini, chopped.
- 2 potatoes.
- 1 leek.
- 1 onion.
- ½ cup olive oil.
- 100g goat cheese.
- 2 carrots.
- Salt and pepper.

**Directions.**

- Put the ingredients in a bag and seal. Set to cook in the water bath for  hours.
- Transfer and mash the potatoes.
- Season and serve

**Nutritional value.**

**Calories 32**

**Protein 2.42g**

**Carbs 6.75g**

**Fat. 0.36g**

# Bone Broth.

**Servings 2**

**Prep time.5 minutes.**

**Cooking time. 1 hour.**

**Ingredients.**

- 200g assorted bones.
- 2 leeks.
- 1 carrot.
- Salt and pepper.
- 2 cups of water.
- Red boat fish sauce.

**Directions.**

- Toss the bones and vegetables in the pouch and set to cook for 1 hour in the water bath at 67C.
- transfer, strain the broth and serve.

**Nutritional value.**

**Calories. 120**

**Proteins 13.20g**

**Fat. 6.1g**

**Carbs 0g**

# Onion Soup

**Servings.2**

**Prep time.10 minutes**

**Cooking time. 4 hours.**

**Ingredients.**

- 200g pork stock.
- 2 cups yellow onion.
- 2tbsp thyme.
- Salt to taste.
- 2 bay leaves,
- Balsamic vinegar.

**Directions.**

- Put all ingredients in a bag and seal. Set to cook for 4 hours in the water bath at 77C.
- Discard the bay leaves and add some seasoning.
- Serve as desired.

**Nutritional value.**

**Calories.369**

**Fat. 16.51g**

**Protein.15.21g**

**Carbs.39.19g**

# Conclusion

Sous vide cooking is by no means a new phenomenon. It has been around for well over a hundred years and is used by chefs at various high-end gourmet restaurants.Sous vide cooking is inexpensive and reasonably simple. The sous vide machine can cook all kinds of food namely, fruits, vegetables, seafood, poultry and meat. Its advantages are most prominent and accentuated when cooking seafood – although seafood could pose the trickiest challenge when using a sous vide cooking machine for the first time. Furthermore, the food has a longer shelf-life, is healthier to eat and easier to make. What is not to like?! The possible slightly longer cook times are easily counterbalanced by the fact that sous vide cooking does not need your undivided attention in the way traditional cooking does. You end up saving a lot more time with sous vide cooking. Whether you want to make that perfect French toast or scrambled eggs, delicious steak or oatmeal, you cannot possibly go wrong with sous vide. Bon appetite!

# ABOUT THE AUTHOR

Amanda Clark is a nutritionist and a professional chef. Amanda spent her entire childhood and part of her teenage years with her grandma. Her grandma taught her all she knew today. Ever since, her love for food has grown to the extent of making her whole life revolve around food. She spends most of her time in the kitchen, trying out new recipes and coming up with new combinations. Beside her love for lies, the second thing she loves most is sharing all she knows about the rest of foodies!

Made in the USA
Middletown, DE
08 September 2017